GRATITUDE JOURNAL
A GUIDED JOURNAL TO CREATING A LIFE OF ABUNDANCE
THROUGH DAILY REFLECTION AND GRATITUDE

BY OPAL M. GRAYSON, LPC

First paperback edition January 2019

Book Cover Image: Pixabay.com

Scripture quotations are from the New International Version.

ISBN 978-1-7928-0058-0 (paperback)

www.gccs-counselingllc.com

CREATE YOUR LIFE OF ABUNDANCE...

Benefits of Gratitude:

Gratitude is the seed for Abundance. Scientific research shows that practicing gratitude will help you to improve your mental, physical, and spiritual wellness. Practicing gratitude can help to improve self-esteem and allow room for healthy relationships in your life. Acknowledging your gratitude can help to empower you and transform your life.

"When you look at life through eyes of gratitude, the world becomes a magical and amazing place."

– Jennifer Gayle

What Do You Get With This Journal?

- Daily Prompts to Help Guide You in Your Reflection

- 30 Positive Affirmations to Help to Empower You and Shift Your Mindset with Positive Thought

- 30 Scriptural References of Gratitude and Abundance for Faith Building and an Increase in Positive Energy

- Photo Areas for Positive Memories

"There is not a more pleasing exercise of the mind than gratitude. It is accompanied with such an inward satisfaction that the duty is sufficiently rewarded by the performance."

~Joseph Addison

This Journal Belongs To:

_____

Personal Reflections

Note: Write At Least One Positive Affirmation or Scriptural Reference of Gratitude/Abundance. Use Daily Prompts/Resources Provided.

Date: 4 / 19 / 19

Arrival today

Scary to put my thoughts to paper but I will give it my best.

"Anyone can find the dirt in someone. It takes someone to find the good.

Personal Reflections

Note: Write At Least One Positive Affirmation or Scriptural Reference of Gratitude/Abundance. Use Daily Prompts/Resources Provided.

Date: 4 /20 / 19

For Gods Blessing en
Keeping us safe during
the storm

I have my whole Easter
dinner ready to go.
Gotta do eggs + ham.

A vigil mass

Dinner @ Outback
with Miah + Poppy

Personal Reflections

Note: Write At Least One Positive Affirmation or Scriptural Reference of Gratitude/Abundance. Use Daily Prompts/Resources Provided.

Date: 4 / 21 / 19

That I awoke this morning

That I have an amazing husband.

I have amazing kids, grand kids & great grand kids.

My body gives me respite from the pain

Do not grieve for the joy of the Lord of the Lord is yours,

Personal Reflections

Note: Write At Least One Positive Affirmation or Scriptural Reference of Gratitude/Abundance. Use Daily Prompts/Resources Provided.

Date: 4/23/19

a long but fruitful
trip to Hatteras

arriving safely

Get my bags
up the stair
with no help

Cleaning and
finishing

Personal Reflections

Note: Write At Least One Positive Affirmation or Scriptural Reference of Gratitude/Abundance. Use Daily Prompts/Resources Provided.

Date: 4 /24/25/ 19

Woke up to Terry Testing their horn @ 630. It works

Condo looks great!

Fact- $125.00 Starting price. Due were $530 we stared here 6 years ago.

Beauty is fully accepting yourself and those around you for exactly what they are. I think there is beauty in absolutely every thing. There is a purpose for every thing, and that can be inspiring

Personal Reflections

Note: Write At Least One Positive Affirmation or Scriptural Reference of Gratitude/Abundance. Use Daily Prompts/Resources Provided.

Date: 5 / 6 / 19

An apology without
Change is just
manipulation

Read that again

Personal Reflections

Note: Write At Least One Positive Affirmation or Scriptural Reference of Gratitude/Abundance. Use Daily Prompts/Resources Provided.

Date: ____/____/____

_____

_____

_____

_____

_____

_____

_____

_____

_____

_____

_____

_____

_____

_____

_____

_____

_____

_____

_____

_____

Personal Reflections

Note: Write At Least One Positive Affirmation or Scriptural Reference of Gratitude/Abundance. Use Daily Prompts/Resources Provided.

Date: ____/____/____

_____

_____

_____

_____

_____

_____

_____

_____

_____

_____

_____

_____

_____

_____

_____

_____

_____

_____

_____

_____

Personal Reflections

Note: Write At Least One Positive Affirmation or Scriptural Reference of Gratitude/Abundance. Use Daily Prompts/Resources Provided.

Date: ____ / ____ / ____

_____

_____

_____

_____

_____

_____

_____

_____

_____

_____

_____

_____

_____

_____

_____

_____

_____

_____

_____

_____

Personal Reflections

Note: Write At Least One Positive Affirmation or Scriptural Reference of Gratitude/Abundance. Use Daily Prompts/Resources Provided.

Date: ____/____/____

_____

_____

_____

_____

_____

_____

_____

_____

_____

_____

_____

_____

_____

_____

_____

_____

_____

_____

_____

_____

_____

Personal Reflections

Note: Write At Least One Positive Affirmation or Scriptural Reference of Gratitude/Abundance. Use Daily Prompts/Resources Provided.

Date: ____/____/____

_____

_____

_____

_____

_____

_____

_____

_____

_____

_____

_____

_____

_____

_____

_____

_____

_____

_____

_____

Personal Reflections

Note: Write At Least One Positive Affirmation or Scriptural Reference of Gratitude/Abundance. Use Daily Prompts/Resources Provided.

Date: ____/____/____

_____

_____

_____

_____

_____

_____

_____

_____

_____

_____

_____

_____

_____

_____

_____

_____

_____

_____

Personal Reflections

Note: Write At Least One Positive Affirmation or Scriptural Reference of Gratitude/Abundance. Use Daily Prompts/Resources Provided.

Date: ____/____/____

_____

_____

_____

_____

_____

_____

_____

_____

_____

_____

_____

_____

_____

_____

_____

_____

_____

_____

_____

Personal Reflections

Note: Write At Least One Positive Affirmation or Scriptural Reference of Gratitude/Abundance. Use Daily Prompts/Resources Provided.

Date: ____/____/____

_____

_____

_____

_____

_____

_____

_____

_____

_____

_____

_____

_____

_____

_____

_____

_____

_____

_____

_____

Personal Reflections

Note: Write At Least One Positive Affirmation or Scriptural Reference of Gratitude/Abundance. Use Daily Prompts/Resources Provided.

Date: ___/___/___

Personal Reflections

Note: Write At Least One Positive Affirmation or Scriptural Reference of Gratitude/Abundance. Use Daily Prompts/Resources Provided.

Date: ____/____/____

_____

_____

_____

_____

_____

_____

_____

_____

_____

_____

_____

_____

_____

_____

_____

_____

_____

_____

_____

Personal Reflections

Note: Write At Least One Positive Affirmation or Scriptural Reference of Gratitude/Abundance. Use Daily Prompts/Resources Provided.

Date: ____/____/____

_____

_____

_____

_____

_____

_____

_____

_____

_____

_____

_____

_____

_____

_____

_____

_____

_____

_____

_____

_____

Personal Reflections

Note: Write At Least One Positive Affirmation or Scriptural Reference of Gratitude/Abundance. Use Daily Prompts/Resources Provided.

Date: ____/____/____

_____

_____

_____

_____

_____

_____

_____

_____

_____

_____

_____

_____

_____

_____

_____

_____

_____

_____

_____

Personal Reflections

Note: Write At Least One Positive Affirmation or Scriptural Reference of Gratitude/Abundance. Use Daily Prompts/Resources Provided.

Date: ____/____/____

_____

_____

_____

_____

_____

_____

_____

_____

_____

_____

_____

_____

_____

_____

_____

_____

_____

_____

_____

_____

_____

Personal Reflections

Note: Write At Least One Positive Affirmation or Scriptural Reference of Gratitude/Abundance. Use Daily Prompts/Resources Provided.

Date: ____ / ____ / ____

_____

_____

_____

_____

_____

_____

_____

_____

_____

_____

_____

_____

_____

_____

_____

_____

_____

_____

_____

Personal Reflections

Note: Write At Least One Positive Affirmation or Scriptural Reference of Gratitude/Abundance. Use Daily Prompts/Resources Provided.

Date: ____ / ____ / ____

_____

_____

_____

_____

_____

_____

_____

_____

_____

_____

_____

_____

_____

_____

_____

_____

_____

_____

_____

Personal Reflections

Note: Write At Least One Positive Affirmation or Scriptural Reference of Gratitude/Abundance. Use Daily Prompts/Resources Provided.

Date: ____/____/____

_____

_____

_____

_____

_____

_____

_____

_____

_____

_____

_____

_____

_____

_____

_____

_____

_____

_____

_____

_____

_____

_____

Personal Reflections

Note: Write At Least One Positive Affirmation or Scriptural Reference of Gratitude/Abundance. Use Daily Prompts/Resources Provided.

Date: ____/____/____

_____

_____

_____

_____

_____

_____

_____

_____

_____

_____

_____

_____

_____

_____

_____

_____

_____

_____

_____

Personal Reflections

Note: Write At Least One Positive Affirmation or Scriptural Reference of Gratitude/Abundance. Use Daily Prompts/Resources Provided.

Date: ___ / ___ / ___

_____

_____

_____

_____

_____

_____

_____

_____

_____

_____

_____

_____

_____

_____

_____

_____

_____

_____

_____

_____

_____

_____

Personal Reflections

Note: Write At Least One Positive Affirmation or Scriptural Reference of Gratitude/Abundance. Use Daily Prompts/Resources Provided.

Date: ____/____/____

_____

_____

_____

_____

_____

_____

_____

_____

_____

_____

_____

_____

_____

_____

_____

_____

_____

_____

_____

_____

Personal Reflections

Note: Write At Least One Positive Affirmation or Scriptural Reference of Gratitude/Abundance. Use Daily Prompts/Resources Provided.

Date: ____/____/____

_____

_____

_____

_____

_____

_____

_____

_____

_____

_____

_____

_____

_____

_____

_____

_____

_____

_____

_____

_____

_____

Personal Reflections

Note: Write At Least One Positive Affirmation or Scriptural Reference of Gratitude/Abundance. Use Daily Prompts/Resources Provided.

Date: ____ / ____ / ____

_____

_____

_____

_____

_____

_____

_____

_____

_____

_____

_____

_____

_____

_____

_____

_____

_____

_____

_____

_____

_____

Personal Reflections

Note: Write At Least One Positive Affirmation or Scriptural Reference of Gratitude/Abundance. Use Daily Prompts/Resources Provided.

Date: _____/_____/_____

Personal Reflections

Note: Write At Least One Positive Affirmation or Scriptural Reference of Gratitude/Abundance. Use Daily Prompts/Resources Provided.

Date: ____/____/____

_____

_____

_____

_____

_____

_____

_____

_____

_____

_____

_____

_____

_____

_____

_____

_____

_____

_____

_____

Personal Reflections

Note: Write At Least One Positive Affirmation or Scriptural Reference of Gratitude/Abundance. Use Daily Prompts/Resources Provided.

Date: ____/____/____

_____

_____

_____

_____

_____

_____

_____

_____

_____

_____

_____

_____

_____

_____

_____

_____

_____

_____

_____

Personal Reflections

Note: Write At Least One Positive Affirmation or Scriptural Reference of Gratitude/Abundance. Use Daily Prompts/Resources Provided.

Date: ____/____/____

Personal Reflections

Note: Write At Least One Positive Affirmation or Scriptural Reference of Gratitude/Abundance. Use Daily Prompts/Resources Provided.

Date: ____/____/____

Personal Reflections

Note: Write At Least One Positive Affirmation or Scriptural Reference of Gratitude/Abundance. Use Daily Prompts/Resources Provided.

Date: ____/____/____

_____

_____

_____

_____

_____

_____

_____

_____

_____

_____

_____

_____

_____

_____

_____

_____

_____

_____

_____

Personal Reflections

Note: Write At Least One Positive Affirmation or Scriptural Reference of Gratitude/Abundance. Use Daily Prompts/Resources Provided.

Date: ____/____/____

_____

_____

_____

_____

_____

_____

_____

_____

_____

_____

_____

_____

_____

_____

_____

_____

_____

_____

_____

_____

Personal Reflections

Note: Write At Least One Positive Affirmation or Scriptural Reference of Gratitude/Abundance. Use Daily Prompts/Resources Provided.

Date: ____ / ____ / ____

_____

_____

_____

_____

_____

_____

_____

_____

_____

_____

_____

_____

_____

_____

_____

_____

_____

_____

_____

Personal Reflections

Note: Write At Least One Positive Affirmation or Scriptural Reference of Gratitude/Abundance. Use Daily Prompts/Resources Provided.

Date: ____/____/____

_____

_____

_____

_____

_____

_____

_____

_____

_____

_____

_____

_____

_____

_____

_____

_____

_____

_____

_____

_____

_____

Personal Reflections

Note: Write At Least One Positive Affirmation or Scriptural Reference of Gratitude/Abundance. Use Daily Prompts/Resources Provided.

Date: ____ / ____ / ____

Personal Reflections

Note: Write At Least One Positive Affirmation or Scriptural Reference of Gratitude/Abundance. Use Daily Prompts/Resources Provided.

Date: ____ / ____ / ____

Personal Reflections

Note: Write At Least One Positive Affirmation or Scriptural Reference of Gratitude/Abundance. Use Daily Prompts/Resources Provided.

Date: ____/____/____

_____

_____

_____

_____

_____

_____

_____

_____

_____

_____

_____

_____

_____

_____

_____

_____

_____

_____

_____

_____

Personal Reflections

Note: Write At Least One Positive Affirmation or Scriptural Reference of Gratitude/Abundance. Use Daily Prompts/Resources Provided.

Date: ____ / ____ / ____

Personal Reflections

Note: Write At Least One Positive Affirmation or Scriptural Reference of Gratitude/Abundance. Use Daily Prompts/Resources Provided.

Date: ____ / ____ / ____

_____

_____

_____

_____

_____

_____

_____

_____

_____

_____

_____

_____

_____

_____

_____

_____

_____

_____

_____

_____

_____

Personal Reflections

Note: Write At Least One Positive Affirmation or Scriptural Reference of Gratitude/Abundance. Use Daily Prompts/Resources Provided.

Date: ____/____/____

_____

_____

_____

_____

_____

_____

_____

_____

_____

_____

_____

_____

_____

_____

_____

_____

_____

_____

_____

_____

Personal Reflections

Note: Write At Least One Positive Affirmation or Scriptural Reference of Gratitude/Abundance. Use Daily Prompts/Resources Provided.

Date: ____/____/____

_____

_____

_____

_____

_____

_____

_____

_____

_____

_____

_____

_____

_____

_____

_____

_____

_____

_____

Personal Reflections

Note: Write At Least One Positive Affirmation or Scriptural Reference of Gratitude/Abundance. Use Daily Prompts/Resources Provided.

Date: ____/____/____

_____

_____

_____

_____

_____

_____

_____

_____

_____

_____

_____

_____

_____

_____

_____

_____

_____

_____

_____

_____

_____

Personal Reflections

Note: Write At Least One Positive Affirmation or Scriptural Reference of Gratitude/Abundance. Use Daily Prompts/Resources Provided.

Date: ____/____/____

_____

_____

_____

_____

_____

_____

_____

_____

_____

_____

_____

_____

_____

_____

_____

_____

_____

_____

_____

_____

Personal Reflections

Note: Write At Least One Positive Affirmation or Scriptural Reference of Gratitude/Abundance. Use Daily Prompts/Resources Provided.

Date: _____/_____/_____

Personal Reflections

Note: Write At Least One Positive Affirmation or Scriptural Reference of Gratitude/Abundance. Use Daily Prompts/Resources Provided.

Date: ____/____/____

_____

_____

_____

_____

_____

_____

_____

_____

_____

_____

_____

_____

_____

_____

_____

_____

_____

_____

_____

_____

Personal Reflections

Note: Write At Least One Positive Affirmation or Scriptural Reference of Gratitude/Abundance. Use Daily Prompts/Resources Provided.

Date: ____/____/____

_____

_____

_____

_____

_____

_____

_____

_____

_____

_____

_____

_____

_____

_____

_____

_____

_____

_____

_____

Personal Reflections

Note: Write At Least One Positive Affirmation or Scriptural Reference of Gratitude/Abundance. Use Daily Prompts/Resources Provided.

Date: _____/_____/_____

Personal Reflections

Note: Write At Least One Positive Affirmation or Scriptural Reference of Gratitude/Abundance. Use Daily Prompts/Resources Provided.

Date: ____/____/____

_____

_____

_____

_____

_____

_____

_____

_____

_____

_____

_____

_____

_____

_____

_____

_____

_____

_____

_____

_____

Personal Reflections

Note: Write At Least One Positive Affirmation or Scriptural Reference of Gratitude/Abundance. Use Daily Prompts/Resources Provided.

Date: ___ / ___ / ___

Personal Reflections

Note: Write At Least One Positive Affirmation or Scriptural Reference of Gratitude/Abundance. Use Daily Prompts/Resources Provided.

Date: ____/____/____

_____

_____

_____

_____

_____

_____

_____

_____

_____

_____

_____

_____

_____

_____

_____

_____

_____

_____

_____

_____

_____

Personal Reflections

Note: Write At Least One Positive Affirmation or Scriptural Reference of Gratitude/Abundance. Use Daily Prompts/Resources Provided.

Date: ____/____/____

Personal Reflections

Note: Write At Least One Positive Affirmation or Scriptural Reference of Gratitude/Abundance. Use Daily Prompts/Resources Provided.

Date: ____/____/____

_____

_____

_____

_____

_____

_____

_____

_____

_____

_____

_____

_____

_____

_____

_____

_____

_____

_____

_____

Personal Reflections

Note: Write At Least One Positive Affirmation or Scriptural Reference of Gratitude/Abundance. Use Daily Prompts/Resources Provided.

Date: ____/____/____

_____

_____

_____

_____

_____

_____

_____

_____

_____

_____

_____

_____

_____

_____

_____

_____

_____

_____

_____

Personal Reflections

Note: Write At Least One Positive Affirmation or Scriptural Reference of Gratitude/Abundance. Use Daily Prompts/Resources Provided.

Date: ____/____/____

_____

_____

_____

_____

_____

_____

_____

_____

_____

_____

_____

_____

_____

_____

_____

_____

_____

_____

_____

_____

_____

_____

Personal Reflections

Note: Write At Least One Positive Affirmation or Scriptural Reference of Gratitude/Abundance. Use Daily Prompts/Resources Provided.

Date: ____ / ____ / ____

_____

_____

_____

_____

_____

_____

_____

_____

_____

_____

_____

_____

_____

_____

_____

_____

_____

_____

Personal Reflections

Note: Write At Least One Positive Affirmation or Scriptural Reference of Gratitude/Abundance. Use Daily Prompts/Resources Provided.

Date: ____/____/____

Personal Reflections

Note: Write At Least One Positive Affirmation or Scriptural Reference of Gratitude/Abundance. Use Daily Prompts/Resources Provided.

Date: ____/____/____

_____

_____

_____

_____

_____

_____

_____

_____

_____

_____

_____

_____

_____

_____

_____

_____

_____

_____

_____

Personal Reflections

Note: Write At Least One Positive Affirmation or Scriptural Reference of Gratitude/Abundance. Use Daily Prompts/Resources Provided.

Date: ____/____/____

_____

_____

_____

_____

_____

_____

_____

_____

_____

_____

_____

_____

_____

_____

_____

_____

_____

_____

_____

_____

Personal Reflections

Note: Write At Least One Positive Affirmation or Scriptural Reference of Gratitude/Abundance. Use Daily Prompts/Resources Provided.

Date: ____ / ____ / ____

_____

_____

_____

_____

_____

_____

_____

_____

_____

_____

_____

_____

_____

_____

_____

_____

_____

_____

_____

Personal Reflections

Note: Write At Least One Positive Affirmation or Scriptural Reference of Gratitude/Abundance. Use Daily Prompts/Resources Provided.

Date: ____/____/____

Personal Reflections

Note: Write At Least One Positive Affirmation or Scriptural Reference of Gratitude/Abundance. Use Daily Prompts/Resources Provided.

Date: ____/____/____

_____

_____

_____

_____

_____

_____

_____

_____

_____

_____

_____

_____

_____

_____

_____

_____

_____

_____

_____

_____

_____

Personal Reflections

Note: Write At Least One Positive Affirmation or Scriptural Reference of Gratitude/Abundance. Use Daily Prompts/Resources Provided.

Date: ____/____/____

Personal Reflections

Note: Write At Least One Positive Affirmation or Scriptural Reference of Gratitude/Abundance. Use Daily Prompts/Resources Provided.

Date: ____ / ____ / ____

_____

_____

_____

_____

_____

_____

_____

_____

_____

_____

_____

_____

_____

_____

_____

_____

_____

_____

_____

Note: Write At Least One Positive Affirmation or Scriptural Reference of Gratitude/Abundance. Use Daily Prompts/Resources Provided.

Date: ____/____/____

_____

_____

_____

_____

_____

_____

_____

_____

_____

_____

_____

_____

_____

_____

_____

_____

_____

_____

_____

_____

_____

Personal Reflections

Note: Write At Least One Positive Affirmation or Scriptural Reference of Gratitude/Abundance. Use Daily Prompts/Resources Provided.

Date: ____ / ____ / ____

_____

_____

_____

_____

_____

_____

_____

_____

_____

_____

_____

_____

_____

_____

_____

_____

_____

_____

_____

Personal Reflections

Note: Write At Least One Positive Affirmation or Scriptural Reference of Gratitude/Abundance. Use Daily Prompts/Resources Provided.

Date: ____ / ____ / ____

_____

_____

_____

_____

_____

_____

_____

_____

_____

_____

_____

_____

_____

_____

_____

_____

_____

_____

_____

_____

Personal Reflections

Note: Write At Least One Positive Affirmation or Scriptural Reference of Gratitude/Abundance. Use Daily Prompts/Resources Provided.

Date: ____/____/____

_____

_____

_____

_____

_____

_____

_____

_____

_____

_____

_____

_____

_____

_____

_____

_____

_____

_____

_____

_____

Personal Reflections

Note: Write At Least One Positive Affirmation or Scriptural Reference of Gratitude/Abundance. Use Daily Prompts/Resources Provided.

Date: ____ / ____ / ____

Personal Reflections

Note: Write At Least One Positive Affirmation or Scriptural Reference of Gratitude/Abundance. Use Daily Prompts/Resources Provided.

Date: ____ / ____ / ____

_____

_____

_____

_____

_____

_____

_____

_____

_____

_____

_____

_____

_____

_____

_____

_____

_____

_____

_____

_____

Personal Reflections

Note: Write At Least One Positive Affirmation or Scriptural Reference of Gratitude/Abundance. Use Daily Prompts/Resources Provided.

Date: ___/___/___

_____

_____

_____

_____

_____

_____

_____

_____

_____

_____

_____

_____

_____

_____

_____

_____

_____

_____

_____

_____

Personal Reflections

Note: Write At Least One Positive Affirmation or Scriptural Reference of Gratitude/Abundance. Use Daily Prompts/Resources Provided.

Date: ____/____/____

_____

_____

_____

_____

_____

_____

_____

_____

_____

_____

_____

_____

_____

_____

_____

_____

_____

_____

_____

_____

Personal Reflections

Note: Write At Least One Positive Affirmation or Scriptural Reference of Gratitude/Abundance. Use Daily Prompts/Resources Provided.

Date: ____/____/____

_____

_____

_____

_____

_____

_____

_____

_____

_____

_____

_____

_____

_____

_____

_____

_____

_____

_____

_____

_____

Personal Reflections

Note: Write At Least One Positive Affirmation or Scriptural Reference of Gratitude/Abundance. Use Daily Prompts/Resources Provided.

Date: ____/____/____

Personal Reflections

Note: Write At Least One Positive Affirmation or Scriptural Reference of Gratitude/Abundance. Use Daily Prompts/Resources Provided.

Date: ____/____/____

_____

_____

_____

_____

_____

_____

_____

_____

_____

_____

_____

_____

_____

_____

_____

_____

_____

_____

_____

_____

Personal Reflections

Note: Write At Least One Positive Affirmation or Scriptural Reference of Gratitude/Abundance. Use Daily Prompts/Resources Provided.

Date: ____/____/____

_____

_____

_____

_____

_____

_____

_____

_____

_____

_____

_____

_____

_____

_____

_____

_____

_____

_____

_____

_____

_____

_____

Personal Reflections

Note: Write At Least One Positive Affirmation or Scriptural Reference of Gratitude/Abundance. Use Daily Prompts/Resources Provided.

Date: ___ / ___ / ___

_____

_____

_____

_____

_____

_____

_____

_____

_____

_____

_____

_____

_____

_____

_____

_____

_____

_____

_____

Personal Reflections

Note: Write At Least One Positive Affirmation or Scriptural Reference of Gratitude/Abundance. Use Daily Prompts/Resources Provided.

Date: ____ / ____ / ____

_____

_____

_____

_____

_____

_____

_____

_____

_____

_____

_____

_____

_____

_____

_____

_____

_____

_____

_____

_____

Personal Reflections

Note: Write At Least One Positive Affirmation or Scriptural Reference of Gratitude/Abundance. Use Daily Prompts/Resources Provided.

Date: ____ / ____ / ____

_____

_____

_____

_____

_____

_____

_____

_____

_____

_____

_____

_____

_____

_____

_____

_____

_____

_____

_____

_____

_____

_____

Personal Reflections

Note: Write At Least One Positive Affirmation or Scriptural Reference of Gratitude/Abundance. Use Daily Prompts/Resources Provided.

Date: ____ / ____ / ____

_____

_____

_____

_____

_____

_____

_____

_____

_____

_____

_____

_____

_____

_____

_____

_____

_____

_____

_____

Personal Reflections

Note: Write At Least One Positive Affirmation or Scriptural Reference of Gratitude/Abundance. Use Daily Prompts/Resources Provided.

Date: ____/____/____

_____

_____

_____

_____

_____

_____

_____

_____

_____

_____

_____

_____

_____

_____

_____

_____

_____

_____

_____

_____

_____

Personal Reflections

Note: Write At Least One Positive Affirmation or Scriptural Reference of Gratitude/Abundance. Use Daily Prompts/Resources Provided.

Date: ____ / ____ / ____

_____

_____

_____

_____

_____

_____

_____

_____

_____

_____

_____

_____

_____

_____

_____

_____

_____

_____

_____

_____

Personal Reflections

Note: Write At Least One Positive Affirmation or Scriptural Reference of Gratitude/Abundance. Use Daily Prompts/Resources Provided.

Date: ____/____/____

_____

_____

_____

_____

_____

_____

_____

_____

_____

_____

_____

_____

_____

_____

_____

_____

_____

_____

_____

_____

Personal Reflections

Note: Write At Least One Positive Affirmation or Scriptural Reference of Gratitude/Abundance. Use Daily Prompts/Resources Provided.

Date: ____/____/____

_____

_____

_____

_____

_____

_____

_____

_____

_____

_____

_____

_____

_____

_____

_____

_____

_____

_____

_____

Personal Reflections

Note: Write At Least One Positive Affirmation or Scriptural Reference of Gratitude/Abundance. Use Daily Prompts/Resources Provided.

Date: ____/____/____

Personal Reflections

Note: Write At Least One Positive Affirmation or Scriptural Reference of Gratitude/Abundance. Use Daily Prompts/Resources Provided.

Date: ____/____/____

_____

_____

_____

_____

_____

_____

_____

_____

_____

_____

_____

_____

_____

_____

_____

_____

_____

_____

_____

Personal Reflections

Note: Write At Least One Positive Affirmation or Scriptural Reference of Gratitude/Abundance. Use Daily Prompts/Resources Provided.

Date: ____/____/____

_____

_____

_____

_____

_____

_____

_____

_____

_____

_____

_____

_____

_____

_____

_____

_____

_____

_____

_____

_____

Personal Reflections

Note: Write At Least One Positive Affirmation or Scriptural Reference of Gratitude/Abundance. Use Daily Prompts/Resources Provided.

Date: ____ / ____ / ____

Personal Reflections

Note: Write At Least One Positive Affirmation or Scriptural Reference of Gratitude/Abundance. Use Daily Prompts/Resources Provided.

Date: ____/____/____

_____

_____

_____

_____

_____

_____

_____

_____

_____

_____

_____

_____

_____

_____

_____

_____

_____

_____

_____

_____

_____

_____

Personal Reflections

Note: Write At Least One Positive Affirmation or Scriptural Reference of Gratitude/Abundance. Use Daily Prompts/Resources Provided.

Date: ____/____/____

_____

_____

_____

_____

_____

_____

_____

_____

_____

_____

_____

_____

_____

_____

_____

_____

_____

_____

_____

Personal Reflections

Note: Write At Least One Positive Affirmation or Scriptural Reference of Gratitude/Abundance. Use Daily Prompts/Resources Provided.

Date: ____/____/____

_____

_____

_____

_____

_____

_____

_____

_____

_____

_____

_____

_____

_____

_____

_____

_____

_____

_____

_____

_____

_____

Personal Reflections

Note: Write At Least One Positive Affirmation or Scriptural Reference of Gratitude/Abundance. Use Daily Prompts/Resources Provided.

Date: ____/____/____

_____

_____

_____

_____

_____

_____

_____

_____

_____

_____

_____

_____

_____

_____

_____

_____

_____

_____

_____

_____

Personal Reflections

Note: Write At Least One Positive Affirmation or Scriptural Reference of Gratitude/Abundance. Use Daily Prompts/Resources Provided.

Date: ____ / ____ / ____

_____

_____

_____

_____

_____

_____

_____

_____

_____

_____

_____

_____

_____

_____

_____

_____

_____

_____

_____

_____

_____

Personal Reflections

Note: Write At Least One Positive Affirmation or Scriptural Reference of Gratitude/Abundance. Use Daily Prompts/Resources Provided.

Date: ____/____/____

Personal Reflections

Note: Write At Least One Positive Affirmation or Scriptural Reference of Gratitude/Abundance. Use Daily Prompts/Resources Provided.

Date: ____/____/____

_____

_____

_____

_____

_____

_____

_____

_____

_____

_____

_____

_____

_____

_____

_____

_____

_____

_____

_____

_____

Personal Reflections

Note: Write At Least One Positive Affirmation or Scriptural Reference of Gratitude/Abundance. Use Daily Prompts/Resources Provided.

Date: ____ / ____ / ____

_____

_____

_____

_____

_____

_____

_____

_____

_____

_____

_____

_____

_____

_____

_____

_____

_____

_____

_____

_____

_____

Personal Reflections

Note: Write At Least One Positive Affirmation or Scriptural Reference of Gratitude/Abundance. Use Daily Prompts/Resources Provided.

Date: ____ / ____ / ____

Personal Reflections

Note: Write At Least One Positive Affirmation or Scriptural Reference of Gratitude/Abundance. Use Daily Prompts/Resources Provided.

Date: ____/____/____

_____

_____

_____

_____

_____

_____

_____

_____

_____

_____

_____

_____

_____

_____

_____

_____

_____

_____

_____

_____

Personal Reflections

Note: Write At Least One Positive Affirmation or Scriptural Reference of Gratitude/Abundance. Use Daily Prompts/Resources Provided.

Date: ____/____/____

_____

_____

_____

_____

_____

_____

_____

_____

_____

_____

_____

_____

_____

_____

_____

_____

_____

_____

_____

_____

_____

Personal Reflections

Note: Write At Least One Positive Affirmation or Scriptural Reference of Gratitude/Abundance. Use Daily Prompts/Resources Provided.

Date: ____/____/____

_____

_____

_____

_____

_____

_____

_____

_____

_____

_____

_____

_____

_____

_____

_____

_____

_____

_____

_____

_____

Personal Reflections

Note: Write At Least One Positive Affirmation or Scriptural Reference of Gratitude/Abundance. Use Daily Prompts/Resources Provided.

Date: ____/____/____

_____

_____

_____

_____

_____

_____

_____

_____

_____

_____

_____

_____

_____

_____

_____

_____

_____

_____

_____

_____

Personal Reflections

Note: Write At Least One Positive Affirmation or Scriptural Reference of Gratitude/Abundance. Use Daily Prompts/Resources Provided.

Date: ___/___/___

_____

_____

_____

_____

_____

_____

_____

_____

_____

_____

_____

_____

_____

_____

_____

_____

_____

_____

Personal Reflections

Note: Write At Least One Positive Affirmation or Scriptural Reference of Gratitude/Abundance. Use Daily Prompts/Resources Provided.

Date: ___ / ___ / ___

_____

_____

_____

_____

_____

_____

_____

_____

_____

_____

_____

_____

_____

_____

_____

_____

_____

_____

_____

_____

_____

_____

Personal Reflections

Note: Write At Least One Positive Affirmation or Scriptural Reference of Gratitude/Abundance. Use Daily Prompts/Resources Provided.

Date: ____/____/____

Date: ____/____/____

_____

_____

_____

_____

_____

_____

_____

_____

_____

_____

_____

_____

_____

_____

_____

_____

_____

_____

_____

_____

_____

Personal Reflections

Note: Write At Least One Positive Affirmation or Scriptural Reference of Gratitude/Abundance. Use Daily Prompts/Resources Provided.

Date: ____ / ____ / ____

Personal Reflections

Note: Write At Least One Positive Affirmation or Scriptural Reference of Gratitude/Abundance. Use Daily Prompts/Resources Provided.

Date: ____/____/____

_____

_____

_____

_____

_____

_____

_____

_____

_____

_____

_____

_____

_____

_____

_____

_____

_____

_____

_____

Personal Reflections

Note: Write At Least One Positive Affirmation or Scriptural Reference of Gratitude/Abundance. Use Daily Prompts/Resources Provided.

Date: ____ / ____ / ____

_____

_____

_____

_____

_____

_____

_____

_____

_____

_____

_____

_____

_____

_____

_____

_____

_____

_____

_____

Personal Reflections

Note: Write At Least One Positive Affirmation or Scriptural Reference of Gratitude/Abundance. Use Daily Prompts/Resources Provided.

Date: ____/____/____

_____

_____

_____

_____

_____

_____

_____

_____

_____

_____

_____

_____

_____

_____

_____

_____

_____

_____

_____

_____

_____

Personal Reflections

Note: Write At Least One Positive Affirmation or Scriptural Reference of Gratitude/Abundance. Use Daily Prompts/Resources Provided.

Date: ____/____/____

Personal Reflections

Note: Write At Least One Positive Affirmation or Scriptural Reference of Gratitude/Abundance. Use Daily Prompts/Resources Provided.

Date: ____/____/____

Personal Reflections

Note: Write At Least One Positive Affirmation or Scriptural Reference of Gratitude/Abundance. Use Daily Prompts/Resources Provided.

Date: ____/____/____

_____

_____

_____

_____

_____

_____

_____

_____

_____

_____

_____

_____

_____

_____

_____

_____

_____

_____

_____

_____

_____

Personal Reflections

Note: Write At Least One Positive Affirmation or Scriptural Reference of Gratitude/Abundance. Use Daily Prompts/Resources Provided.

Date: ____ / ____ / ____

Personal Reflections

Note: Write At Least One Positive Affirmation or Scriptural Reference of Gratitude/Abundance. Use Daily Prompts/Resources Provided.

Date: ____/____/____

_____

_____

_____

_____

_____

_____

_____

_____

_____

_____

_____

_____

_____

_____

_____

_____

_____

_____

_____

_____

_____

Personal Reflections

Note: Write At Least One Positive Affirmation or Scriptural Reference of Gratitude/Abundance. Use Daily Prompts/Resources Provided.

Date: ____ / ____ / ____

_____

_____

_____

_____

_____

_____

_____

_____

_____

_____

_____

_____

_____

_____

_____

_____

_____

_____

_____

Personal Reflections

Note: Write At Least One Positive Affirmation or Scriptural Reference of Gratitude/Abundance. Use Daily Prompts/Resources Provided.

Date: ____ / ____ / ____

_____

_____

_____

_____

_____

_____

_____

_____

_____

_____

_____

_____

_____

_____

_____

_____

_____

_____

Personal Reflections

Note: Write At Least One Positive Affirmation or Scriptural Reference of Gratitude/Abundance. Use Daily Prompts/Resources Provided.

Date: ____/____/____

_____

_____

_____

_____

_____

_____

_____

_____

_____

_____

_____

_____

_____

_____

_____

_____

_____

_____

_____

_____

_____

Personal Reflections

Note: Write At Least One Positive Affirmation or Scriptural Reference of Gratitude/Abundance. Use Daily Prompts/Resources Provided.

Date: ____/____/____

Personal Reflections

Note: Write At Least One Positive Affirmation or Scriptural Reference of Gratitude/Abundance. Use Daily Prompts/Resources Provided.

Date: ____/____/____

_____

_____

_____

_____

_____

_____

_____

_____

_____

_____

_____

_____

_____

_____

_____

_____

_____

_____

_____

_____

Personal Reflections

Note: Write At Least One Positive Affirmation or Scriptural Reference of Gratitude/Abundance. Use Daily Prompts/Resources Provided.

Date: ____ / ____ / ____

Personal Reflections

Note: Write At Least One Positive Affirmation or Scriptural Reference of Gratitude/Abundance. Use Daily Prompts/Resources Provided.

Date: ____/____/____

_____

_____

_____

_____

_____

_____

_____

_____

_____

_____

_____

_____

_____

_____

_____

_____

_____

_____

_____

_____

Personal Reflections

Note: Write At Least One Positive Affirmation or Scriptural Reference of Gratitude/Abundance. Use Daily Prompts/Resources Provided.

Date: ___ / ___ / ___

_____

_____

_____

_____

_____

_____

_____

_____

_____

_____

_____

_____

_____

_____

_____

_____

_____

_____

_____

_____

_____

Personal Reflections

Note: Write At Least One Positive Affirmation or Scriptural Reference of Gratitude/Abundance. Use Daily Prompts/Resources Provided.

Date: ____ / ____ / ____

_____

_____

_____

_____

_____

_____

_____

_____

_____

_____

_____

_____

_____

_____

_____

_____

_____

_____

_____

_____

Personal Reflections

Note: Write At Least One Positive Affirmation or Scriptural Reference of Gratitude/Abundance. Use Daily Prompts/Resources Provided.

Date: ____/____/____

_____

_____

_____

_____

_____

_____

_____

_____

_____

_____

_____

_____

_____

_____

_____

_____

_____

_____

_____

_____

Personal Reflections

Note: Write At Least One Positive Affirmation or Scriptural Reference of Gratitude/Abundance. Use Daily Prompts/Resources Provided.

Date: ____/____/____

_____

_____

_____

_____

_____

_____

_____

_____

_____

_____

_____

_____

_____

_____

_____

_____

_____

_____

_____

_____

Personal Reflections

Note: Write At Least One Positive Affirmation or Scriptural Reference of Gratitude/Abundance. Use Daily Prompts/Resources Provided.

Date: ____/____/____

Personal Reflections

Note: Write At Least One Positive Affirmation or Scriptural Reference of Gratitude/Abundance. Use Daily Prompts/Resources Provided.

Date: ____/____/____

_____

_____

_____

_____

_____

_____

_____

_____

_____

_____

_____

_____

_____

_____

_____

_____

_____

_____

_____

Personal Reflections

Note: Write At Least One Positive Affirmation or Scriptural Reference of Gratitude/Abundance. Use Daily Prompts/Resources Provided.

Date: ____/____/____

_____

_____

_____

_____

_____

_____

_____

_____

_____

_____

_____

_____

_____

_____

_____

_____

_____

_____

_____

Personal Reflections

Note: Write At Least One Positive Affirmation or Scriptural Reference of Gratitude/Abundance. Use Daily Prompts/Resources Provided.

Date: ____/____/____

_____

_____

_____

_____

_____

_____

_____

_____

_____

_____

_____

_____

_____

_____

_____

_____

_____

_____

_____

_____

Personal Reflections

Note: Write At Least One Positive Affirmation or Scriptural Reference of Gratitude/Abundance. Use Daily Prompts/Resources Provided.

Date: ____/____/____

_____

_____

_____

_____

_____

_____

_____

_____

_____

_____

_____

_____

_____

_____

_____

_____

_____

_____

_____

_____

_____

Personal Reflections

Note: Write At Least One Positive Affirmation or Scriptural Reference of Gratitude/Abundance. Use Daily Prompts/Resources Provided.

Date: ____/____/____

_____

_____

_____

_____

_____

_____

_____

_____

_____

_____

_____

_____

_____

_____

_____

_____

_____

_____

Personal Reflections

Note: Write At Least One Positive Affirmation or Scriptural Reference of Gratitude/Abundance. Use Daily Prompts/Resources Provided.

Date: ___ / ___ / ___

_____

_____

_____

_____

_____

_____

_____

_____

_____

_____

_____

_____

_____

_____

_____

_____

_____

_____

_____

Personal Reflections

Note: Write At Least One Positive Affirmation or Scriptural Reference of Gratitude/Abundance. Use Daily Prompts/Resources Provided.

Date: ____/____/____

Personal Reflections

Note: Write At Least One Positive Affirmation or Scriptural Reference of Gratitude/Abundance. Use Daily Prompts/Resources Provided.

Date: ____/____/____

_____

_____

_____

_____

_____

_____

_____

_____

_____

_____

_____

_____

_____

_____

_____

_____

_____

_____

_____

_____

_____

Personal Reflections

Note: Write At Least One Positive Affirmation or Scriptural Reference of Gratitude/Abundance. Use Daily Prompts/Resources Provided.

Date: ____/____/____

_____

_____

_____

_____

_____

_____

_____

_____

_____

_____

_____

_____

_____

_____

_____

_____

_____

_____

_____

_____

Personal Reflections

Note: Write At Least One Positive Affirmation or Scriptural Reference of Gratitude/Abundance. Use Daily Prompts/Resources Provided.

Date: ____/____/____

_____

_____

_____

_____

_____

_____

_____

_____

_____

_____

_____

_____

_____

_____

_____

_____

_____

_____

_____

_____

_____

_____

Personal Reflections

Note: Write At Least One Positive Affirmation or Scriptural Reference of Gratitude/Abundance. Use Daily Prompts/Resources Provided.

Date: ____/____/____

_____

_____

_____

_____

_____

_____

_____

_____

_____

_____

_____

_____

_____

_____

_____

_____

_____

_____

_____

_____

_____

_____

Personal Reflections

Note: Write At Least One Positive Affirmation or Scriptural Reference of Gratitude/Abundance. Use Daily Prompts/Resources Provided.

Date: ____/____/____

_____

_____

_____

_____

_____

_____

_____

_____

_____

_____

_____

_____

_____

_____

_____

_____

_____

_____

_____

_____

Personal Reflections

Note: Write At Least One Positive Affirmation or Scriptural Reference of Gratitude/Abundance. Use Daily Prompts/Resources Provided.

Date: ____/____/____

_____

_____

_____

_____

_____

_____

_____

_____

_____

_____

_____

_____

_____

_____

_____

_____

_____

_____

_____

_____

_____

Personal Reflections

Note: Write At Least One Positive Affirmation or Scriptural Reference of Gratitude/Abundance. Use Daily Prompts/Resources Provided.

Date: ____/____/____

_____

_____

_____

_____

_____

_____

_____

_____

_____

_____

_____

_____

_____

_____

_____

_____

_____

_____

_____

_____

_____

Personal Reflections

Note: Write At Least One Positive Affirmation or Scriptural Reference of Gratitude/Abundance. Use Daily Prompts/Resources Provided.

Date: ____/____/____

_____

_____

_____

_____

_____

_____

_____

_____

_____

_____

_____

_____

_____

_____

_____

_____

_____

_____

_____

_____

Personal Reflections

Note: Write At Least One Positive Affirmation or Scriptural Reference of Gratitude/Abundance. Use Daily Prompts/Resources Provided.

Date: ___ / ___ / ___

Personal Reflections

Note: Write At Least One Positive Affirmation or Scriptural Reference of Gratitude/Abundance. Use Daily Prompts/Resources Provided.

Date: ___ / ___ / ___

_____

_____

_____

_____

_____

_____

_____

_____

_____

_____

_____

_____

_____

_____

_____

_____

_____

_____

_____

_____

Personal Reflections

Note: Write At Least One Positive Affirmation or Scriptural Reference of Gratitude/Abundance. Use Daily Prompts/Resources Provided.

Date: ____/____/____

Personal Reflections

Note: Write At Least One Positive Affirmation or Scriptural Reference of Gratitude/Abundance. Use Daily Prompts/Resources Provided.

Date: ____/____/____

_____

_____

_____

_____

_____

_____

_____

_____

_____

_____

_____

_____

_____

_____

_____

_____

_____

_____

_____

_____

_____

Personal Reflections

Note: Write At Least One Positive Affirmation or Scriptural Reference of Gratitude/Abundance. Use Daily Prompts/Resources Provided.

Date: ____/____/____

_____

_____

_____

_____

_____

_____

_____

_____

_____

_____

_____

_____

_____

_____

_____

_____

_____

_____

_____

_____

_____

Personal Reflections

Note: Write At Least One Positive Affirmation or Scriptural Reference of Gratitude/Abundance. Use Daily Prompts/Resources Provided.

Date: ____/____/____

Personal Reflections

Note: Write At Least One Positive Affirmation or Scriptural Reference of Gratitude/Abundance. Use Daily Prompts/Resources Provided.

Date: ____/____/____

_____

_____

_____

_____

_____

_____

_____

_____

_____

_____

_____

_____

_____

_____

_____

_____

_____

_____

_____

_____

_____

_____

Personal Reflections

Note: Write At Least One Positive Affirmation or Scriptural Reference of Gratitude/Abundance. Use Daily Prompts/Resources Provided.

Date: ____/____/____

_____

_____

_____

_____

_____

_____

_____

_____

_____

_____

_____

_____

_____

_____

_____

_____

_____

_____

_____

_____

_____

Personal Reflections

Note: Write At Least One Positive Affirmation or Scriptural Reference of Gratitude/Abundance. Use Daily Prompts/Resources Provided.

Date: ____ / ____ / ____

_____

_____

_____

_____

_____

_____

_____

_____

_____

_____

_____

_____

_____

_____

_____

_____

_____

_____

_____

_____

_____

Personal Reflections

Note: Write At Least One Positive Affirmation or Scriptural Reference of Gratitude/Abundance. Use Daily Prompts/Resources Provided.

Date: ____/____/____

_____

_____

_____

_____

_____

_____

_____

_____

_____

_____

_____

_____

_____

_____

_____

_____

_____

_____

_____

_____

Personal Reflections

Note: Write At Least One Positive Affirmation or Scriptural Reference of Gratitude/Abundance. Use Daily Prompts/Resources Provided.

Date: ____ / ____ / ____

_____

_____

_____

_____

_____

_____

_____

_____

_____

_____

_____

_____

_____

_____

_____

_____

_____

_____

_____

_____

_____

_____

_____

Personal Reflections

Note: Write At Least One Positive Affirmation or Scriptural Reference of Gratitude/Abundance. Use Daily Prompts/Resources Provided.

Date: ____ / ____ / ____

_____

_____

_____

_____

_____

_____

_____

_____

_____

_____

_____

_____

_____

_____

_____

_____

_____

_____

_____

_____

Personal Reflections

Note: Write At Least One Positive Affirmation or Scriptural Reference of Gratitude/Abundance. Use Daily Prompts/Resources Provided.

Date: ____/____/____

_____

_____

_____

_____

_____

_____

_____

_____

_____

_____

_____

_____

_____

_____

_____

_____

_____

_____

_____

_____

Personal Reflections

Note: Write At Least One Positive Affirmation or Scriptural Reference of Gratitude/Abundance. Use Daily Prompts/Resources Provided.

Date: ____/____/____

Personal Reflections

Note: Write At Least One Positive Affirmation or Scriptural Reference of Gratitude/Abundance. Use Daily Prompts/Resources Provided.

Date: ____/____/____

_____

_____

_____

_____

_____

_____

_____

_____

_____

_____

_____

_____

_____

_____

_____

_____

_____

_____

_____

_____

_____

Personal Reflections

Note: Write At Least One Positive Affirmation or Scriptural Reference of Gratitude/Abundance. Use Daily Prompts/Resources Provided.

Date: ____ / ____ / ____

Personal Reflections

Note: Write At Least One Positive Affirmation or Scriptural Reference of Gratitude/Abundance. Use Daily Prompts/Resources Provided.

Date: ____/____/____

_____

_____

_____

_____

_____

_____

_____

_____

_____

_____

_____

_____

_____

_____

_____

_____

_____

_____

Personal Reflections

Note: Write At Least One Positive Affirmation or Scriptural Reference of Gratitude/Abundance. Use Daily Prompts/Resources Provided.

Date: ____ / ____ / ____

_____

_____

_____

_____

_____

_____

_____

_____

_____

_____

_____

_____

_____

_____

_____

_____

_____

_____

_____

_____

_____

Personal Reflections

Note: Write At Least One Positive Affirmation or Scriptural Reference of Gratitude/Abundance. Use Daily Prompts/Resources Provided.

Date: ____/____/____

_____

_____

_____

_____

_____

_____

_____

_____

_____

_____

_____

_____

_____

_____

_____

_____

_____

_____

_____

_____

Personal Reflections

Note: Write At Least One Positive Affirmation or Scriptural Reference of Gratitude/Abundance. Use Daily Prompts/Resources Provided.

Date: ____/____/____

_____

_____

_____

_____

_____

_____

_____

_____

_____

_____

_____

_____

_____

_____

_____

_____

_____

_____

_____

Personal Reflections

Note: Write At Least One Positive Affirmation or Scriptural Reference of Gratitude/Abundance. Use Daily Prompts/Resources Provided.

Date: ____/____/____

_____

_____

_____

_____

_____

_____

_____

_____

_____

_____

_____

_____

_____

_____

_____

_____

_____

_____

_____

_____

Personal Reflections

Note: Write At Least One Positive Affirmation or Scriptural Reference of Gratitude/Abundance. Use Daily Prompts/Resources Provided.

Date: ____ / ____ / ____

_____

_____

_____

_____

_____

_____

_____

_____

_____

_____

_____

_____

_____

_____

_____

_____

_____

_____

_____

_____

Personal Reflections

Note: Write At Least One Positive Affirmation or Scriptural Reference of Gratitude/Abundance. Use Daily Prompts/Resources Provided.

Date: ____ / ____ / ____

_____

_____

_____

_____

_____

_____

_____

_____

_____

_____

_____

_____

_____

_____

_____

_____

_____

_____

_____

_____

Personal Reflections

Note: Write At Least One Positive Affirmation or Scriptural Reference of Gratitude/Abundance. Use Daily Prompts/Resources Provided.

Date: ____/____/____

_____

_____

_____

_____

_____

_____

_____

_____

_____

_____

_____

_____

_____

_____

_____

_____

_____

_____

_____

_____

Personal Reflections

Note: Write At Least One Positive Affirmation or Scriptural Reference of Gratitude/Abundance. Use Daily Prompts/Resources Provided.

Date: ____ / ____ / ____

_____

_____

_____

_____

_____

_____

_____

_____

_____

_____

_____

_____

_____

_____

_____

_____

_____

_____

_____

_____

_____

_____

Personal Reflections

Note: Write At Least One Positive Affirmation or Scriptural Reference of Gratitude/Abundance. Use Daily Prompts/Resources Provided.

Date: _____ / _____ / _____

_____

_____

_____

_____

_____

_____

_____

_____

_____

_____

_____

_____

_____

_____

_____

_____

_____

_____

_____

_____

_____

Personal Reflections

Note: Write At Least One Positive Affirmation or Scriptural Reference of Gratitude/Abundance. Use Daily Prompts/Resources Provided.

Date: ____/____/____

Personal Reflections

Note: Write At Least One Positive Affirmation or Scriptural Reference of Gratitude/Abundance. Use Daily Prompts/Resources Provided.

Date: ____/____/____

Personal Reflections

Note: Write At Least One Positive Affirmation or Scriptural Reference of Gratitude/Abundance. Use Daily Prompts/Resources Provided.

Date: ____ / ____ / ____

_____

_____

_____

_____

_____

_____

_____

_____

_____

_____

_____

_____

_____

_____

_____

_____

_____

_____

_____

Personal Reflections

Note: Write At Least One Positive Affirmation or Scriptural Reference of Gratitude/Abundance. Use Daily Prompts/Resources Provided.

Date: ____/____/____

_____

_____

_____

_____

_____

_____

_____

_____

_____

_____

_____

_____

_____

_____

_____

_____

_____

_____

_____

_____

_____

Personal Reflections

Note: Write At Least One Positive Affirmation or Scriptural Reference of Gratitude/Abundance. Use Daily Prompts/Resources Provided.

Date: ___ / ___ / ___

_____

_____

_____

_____

_____

_____

_____

_____

_____

_____

_____

_____

_____

_____

_____

_____

_____

_____

_____

_____

_____

Personal Reflections

Note: Write At Least One Positive Affirmation or Scriptural Reference of Gratitude/Abundance. Use Daily Prompts/Resources Provided.

Date: ____/____/____

_____

_____

_____

_____

_____

_____

_____

_____

_____

_____

_____

_____

_____

_____

_____

_____

_____

_____

_____

_____

Personal Reflections

Note: Write At Least One Positive Affirmation or Scriptural Reference of Gratitude/Abundance. Use Daily Prompts/Resources Provided.

Date: ____/____/____

_____

_____

_____

_____

_____

_____

_____

_____

_____

_____

_____

_____

_____

_____

_____

_____

_____

_____

_____

_____

_____

_____

Personal Reflections

Note: Write At Least One Positive Affirmation or Scriptural Reference of Gratitude/Abundance. Use Daily Prompts/Resources Provided.

Date: ____/____/____

_____

_____

_____

_____

_____

_____

_____

_____

_____

_____

_____

_____

_____

_____

_____

_____

_____

_____

_____

_____

_____

_____

Personal Reflections

Note: Write At Least One Positive Affirmation or Scriptural Reference of Gratitude/Abundance. Use Daily Prompts/Resources Provided.

Date: ____ / ____ / ____

_____

_____

_____

_____

_____

_____

_____

_____

_____

_____

_____

_____

_____

_____

_____

_____

_____

_____

_____

_____

_____

Personal Reflections

Note: Write At Least One Positive Affirmation or Scriptural Reference of Gratitude/Abundance. Use Daily Prompts/Resources Provided.

Date: ____/____/____

_____

_____

_____

_____

_____

_____

_____

_____

_____

_____

_____

_____

_____

_____

_____

_____

_____

_____

_____

_____

Personal Reflections

Note: Write At Least One Positive Affirmation or Scriptural Reference of Gratitude/Abundance. Use Daily Prompts/Resources Provided.

Date: ____ / ____ / ____

_____

_____

_____

_____

_____

_____

_____

_____

_____

_____

_____

_____

_____

_____

_____

_____

_____

_____

_____

_____

_____

_____

Personal Reflections

Note: Write At Least One Positive Affirmation or Scriptural Reference of Gratitude/Abundance. Use Daily Prompts/Resources Provided.

Date: ____/____/____

_____

_____

_____

_____

_____

_____

_____

_____

_____

_____

_____

_____

_____

_____

_____

_____

_____

_____

_____

_____

Personal Reflections

Note: Write At Least One Positive Affirmation or Scriptural Reference of Gratitude/Abundance. Use Daily Prompts/Resources Provided.

Date: ____/____/____

_____

_____

_____

_____

_____

_____

_____

_____

_____

_____

_____

_____

_____

_____

_____

_____

_____

_____

_____

Personal Reflections

Note: Write At Least One Positive Affirmation or Scriptural Reference of Gratitude/Abundance. Use Daily Prompts/Resources Provided.

Date: ____ / ____ / ____

_____

_____

_____

_____

_____

_____

_____

_____

_____

_____

_____

_____

_____

_____

_____

_____

_____

_____

Personal Reflections

Note: Write At Least One Positive Affirmation or Scriptural Reference of Gratitude/Abundance. Use Daily Prompts/Resources Provided.

Date: ____ / ____ / ____

Personal Reflections

Note: Write At Least One Positive Affirmation or Scriptural Reference of Gratitude/Abundance. Use Daily Prompts/Resources Provided.

Date: ____/____/____

_____

_____

_____

_____

_____

_____

_____

_____

_____

_____

_____

_____

_____

_____

_____

_____

_____

_____

_____

_____

Personal Reflections

Note: Write At Least One Positive Affirmation or Scriptural Reference of Gratitude/Abundance. Use Daily Prompts/Resources Provided.

Date: ____/____/____

_____

_____

_____

_____

_____

_____

_____

_____

_____

_____

_____

_____

_____

_____

_____

_____

_____

_____

_____

_____

_____

_____

_____

Personal Reflections

Note: Write At Least One Positive Affirmation or Scriptural Reference of Gratitude/Abundance. Use Daily Prompts/Resources Provided.

Date: ____/____/____

Personal Reflections

Note: Write At Least One Positive Affirmation or Scriptural Reference of Gratitude/Abundance. Use Daily Prompts/Resources Provided.

Date: ____/____/____

_____

_____

_____

_____

_____

_____

_____

_____

_____

_____

_____

_____

_____

_____

_____

_____

_____

_____

_____

_____

_____

Personal Reflections

Note: Write At Least One Positive Affirmation or Scriptural Reference of Gratitude/Abundance. Use Daily Prompts/Resources Provided.

Date: ____ / ____ / ____

_____

_____

_____

_____

_____

_____

_____

_____

_____

_____

_____

_____

_____

_____

_____

_____

_____

_____

_____

_____

_____

Personal Reflections

Note: Write At Least One Positive Affirmation or Scriptural Reference of Gratitude/Abundance. Use Daily Prompts/Resources Provided.

Date: ____/____/____

Personal Reflections

Note: Write At Least One Positive Affirmation or Scriptural Reference of Gratitude/Abundance. Use Daily Prompts/Resources Provided.

Date: ____/____/____

_____

_____

_____

_____

_____

_____

_____

_____

_____

_____

_____

_____

_____

_____

_____

_____

_____

_____

_____

_____

_____

Personal Reflections

Note: Write At Least One Positive Affirmation or Scriptural Reference of Gratitude/Abundance. Use Daily Prompts/Resources Provided.

Date: ____ / ____ / ____

_____

_____

_____

_____

_____

_____

_____

_____

_____

_____

_____

_____

_____

_____

_____

_____

_____

_____

_____

_____

_____

_____

Personal Reflections

Note: Write At Least One Positive Affirmation or Scriptural Reference of Gratitude/Abundance. Use Daily Prompts/Resources Provided.

Date: ____/____/____

Personal Reflections

Note: Write At Least One Positive Affirmation or Scriptural Reference of Gratitude/Abundance. Use Daily Prompts/Resources Provided.

Date: ____ / ____ / ____

Personal Reflections

Note: Write At Least One Positive Affirmation or Scriptural Reference of Gratitude/Abundance. Use Daily Prompts/Resources Provided.

Date: ____/____/____

Personal Reflections

Note: Write At Least One Positive Affirmation or Scriptural Reference of Gratitude/Abundance. Use Daily Prompts/Resources Provided.

Date: ____ / ____ / ____

_____

_____

_____

_____

_____

_____

_____

_____

_____

_____

_____

_____

_____

_____

_____

_____

_____

_____

_____

_____

_____

Personal Reflections

Note: Write At Least One Positive Affirmation or Scriptural Reference of Gratitude/Abundance. Use Daily Prompts/Resources Provided.

Date: ____/____/____

_____

_____

_____

_____

_____

_____

_____

_____

_____

_____

_____

_____

_____

_____

_____

_____

_____

_____

_____

_____

_____

Personal Reflections

Note: Write At Least One Positive Affirmation or Scriptural Reference of Gratitude/Abundance. Use Daily Prompts/Resources Provided.

Date: ____ / ____ / ____

Personal Reflections

Note: Write At Least One Positive Affirmation or Scriptural Reference of Gratitude/Abundance. Use Daily Prompts/Resources Provided.

Date: ____/____/____

Personal Reflections

Note: Write At Least One Positive Affirmation or Scriptural Reference of Gratitude/Abundance. Use Daily Prompts/Resources Provided.

Date: ____ / ____ / ____

_____

_____

_____

_____

_____

_____

_____

_____

_____

_____

_____

_____

_____

_____

_____

_____

_____

_____

_____

_____

_____

Personal Reflections

Note: Write At Least One Positive Affirmation or Scriptural Reference of Gratitude/Abundance. Use Daily Prompts/Resources Provided.

Date: ____/____/____

_____

_____

_____

_____

_____

_____

_____

_____

_____

_____

_____

_____

_____

_____

_____

_____

_____

_____

_____

Personal Reflections

Note: Write At Least One Positive Affirmation or Scriptural Reference of Gratitude/Abundance. Use Daily Prompts/Resources Provided.

Date: ____/____/____

_____

_____

_____

_____

_____

_____

_____

_____

_____

_____

_____

_____

_____

_____

_____

_____

_____

_____

_____

_____

Date: ____/____/____

_____

_____

_____

_____

_____

_____

_____

_____

_____

_____

_____

_____

_____

_____

_____

_____

_____

_____

_____

_____

_____

Personal Reflections

Note: Write At Least One Positive Affirmation or Scriptural Reference of Gratitude/Abundance. Use Daily Prompts/Resources Provided.

Date: ____/____/____

_____

_____

_____

_____

_____

_____

_____

_____

_____

_____

_____

_____

_____

_____

_____

_____

_____

_____

_____

_____

_____

Personal Reflections

Note: Write At Least One Positive Affirmation or Scriptural Reference of Gratitude/Abundance. Use Daily Prompts/Resources Provided.

Date: ____ / ____ / ____

_____

_____

_____

_____

_____

_____

_____

_____

_____

_____

_____

_____

_____

_____

_____

_____

_____

_____

_____

_____

Personal Reflections

Note: Write At Least One Positive Affirmation or Scriptural Reference of Gratitude/Abundance. Use Daily Prompts/Resources Provided.

Date: ____ / ____ / ____

_____

_____

_____

_____

_____

_____

_____

_____

_____

_____

_____

_____

_____

_____

_____

_____

_____

_____

_____

_____

_____

_____

Personal Reflections

Note: Write At Least One Positive Affirmation or Scriptural Reference of Gratitude/Abundance. Use Daily Prompts/Resources Provided.

Date: ____/____/____

_____

_____

_____

_____

_____

_____

_____

_____

_____

_____

_____

_____

_____

_____

_____

_____

_____

_____

_____

_____

Personal Reflections

Note: Write At Least One Positive Affirmation or Scriptural Reference of Gratitude/Abundance. Use Daily Prompts/Resources Provided.

Date: ____ / ____ / ____

_____

_____

_____

_____

_____

_____

_____

_____

_____

_____

_____

_____

_____

_____

_____

_____

_____

_____

_____

_____

Personal Reflections

Note: Write At Least One Positive Affirmation or Scriptural Reference of Gratitude/Abundance. Use Daily Prompts/Resources Provided.

Date: ____/____/____

_____

_____

_____

_____

_____

_____

_____

_____

_____

_____

_____

_____

_____

_____

_____

_____

_____

_____

_____

Note: Write At Least One Positive Affirmation or Scriptural Reference of Gratitude/Abundance. Use Daily Prompts/Resources Provided.

Date: ____/____/____

_____

_____

_____

_____

_____

_____

_____

_____

_____

_____

_____

_____

_____

_____

_____

_____

_____

_____

_____

Personal Reflections

Note: Write At Least One Positive Affirmation or Scriptural Reference of Gratitude/Abundance. Use Daily Prompts/Resources Provided.

Date: ____/____/____

_____

_____

_____

_____

_____

_____

_____

_____

_____

_____

_____

_____

_____

_____

_____

_____

_____

_____

_____

_____

Personal Reflections

Note: Write At Least One Positive Affirmation or Scriptural Reference of Gratitude/Abundance. Use Daily Prompts/Resources Provided.

Date: ____/____/____

_____

_____

_____

_____

_____

_____

_____

_____

_____

_____

_____

_____

_____

_____

_____

_____

_____

_____

_____

_____

_____

Personal Reflections

Note: Write At Least One Positive Affirmation or Scriptural Reference of Gratitude/Abundance. Use Daily Prompts/Resources Provided.

Date: ____/____/____

Personal Reflections

Note: Write At Least One Positive Affirmation or Scriptural Reference of Gratitude/Abundance. Use Daily Prompts/Resources Provided.

Date: ____ / ____ / ____

_____

_____

_____

_____

_____

_____

_____

_____

_____

_____

_____

_____

_____

_____

_____

_____

_____

_____

_____

_____

_____

_____

Personal Reflections

Note: Write At Least One Positive Affirmation or Scriptural Reference of Gratitude/Abundance. Use Daily Prompts/Resources Provided.

Date: ____ / ____ / ____

_____

_____

_____

_____

_____

_____

_____

_____

_____

_____

_____

_____

_____

_____

_____

_____

_____

_____

_____

_____

_____

Personal Reflections

Note: Write At Least One Positive Affirmation or Scriptural Reference of Gratitude/Abundance. Use Daily Prompts/Resources Provided.

Date: ____ / ____ / ____

_____

_____

_____

_____

_____

_____

_____

_____

_____

_____

_____

_____

_____

_____

_____

_____

_____

_____

_____

_____

_____

Date: ___ / ___ / ___

_____

_____

_____

_____

_____

_____

_____

_____

_____

_____

_____

_____

_____

_____

_____

_____

_____

_____

Personal Reflections

Note: Write At Least One Positive Affirmation or Scriptural Reference of Gratitude/Abundance. Use Daily Prompts/Resources Provided.

Date: ____ / ____ / ____

_____

_____

_____

_____

_____

_____

_____

_____

_____

_____

_____

_____

_____

_____

_____

_____

_____

_____

_____

_____

_____

Personal Reflections

Note: Write At Least One Positive Affirmation or Scriptural Reference of Gratitude/Abundance. Use Daily Prompts/Resources Provided.

Date: ____/____/____

_____

_____

_____

_____

_____

_____

_____

_____

_____

_____

_____

_____

_____

_____

_____

_____

_____

_____

_____

_____

Personal Reflections

Note: Write At Least One Positive Affirmation or Scriptural Reference of Gratitude/Abundance. Use Daily Prompts/Resources Provided.

Date: ____/____/____

_____

_____

_____

_____

_____

_____

_____

_____

_____

_____

_____

_____

_____

_____

_____

_____

_____

_____

_____

_____

_____

_____

Personal Reflections

Note: Write At Least One Positive Affirmation or Scriptural Reference of Gratitude/Abundance. Use Daily Prompts/Resources Provided.

Date: ____/____/____

_____

_____

_____

_____

_____

_____

_____

_____

_____

_____

_____

_____

_____

_____

_____

_____

_____

_____

_____

_____

_____

Personal Reflections

Note: Write At Least One Positive Affirmation or Scriptural Reference of Gratitude/Abundance. Use Daily Prompts/Resources Provided.

Date: ___ / ___ / ___

_____

_____

_____

_____

_____

_____

_____

_____

_____

_____

_____

_____

_____

_____

_____

_____

_____

_____

_____

_____

_____

Personal Reflections

Note: Write At Least One Positive Affirmation or Scriptural Reference of Gratitude/Abundance. Use Daily Prompts/Resources Provided.

Date: ____ / ____ / ____

_____

_____

_____

_____

_____

_____

_____

_____

_____

_____

_____

_____

_____

_____

_____

_____

_____

_____

Personal Reflections

Note: Write At Least One Positive Affirmation or Scriptural Reference of Gratitude/Abundance. Use Daily Prompts/Resources Provided.

Date: ____ / ____ / ____

_____

_____

_____

_____

_____

_____

_____

_____

_____

_____

_____

_____

_____

_____

_____

_____

_____

_____

_____

_____

_____

Personal Reflections

Note: Write At Least One Positive Affirmation or Scriptural Reference of Gratitude/Abundance. Use Daily Prompts/Resources Provided.

Date: ___ / ___ / ___

_____

_____

_____

_____

_____

_____

_____

_____

_____

_____

_____

_____

_____

_____

_____

_____

_____

_____

_____

_____

Personal Reflections

Note: Write At Least One Positive Affirmation or Scriptural Reference of Gratitude/Abundance. Use Daily Prompts/Resources Provided.

Date: ____ / ____ / ____

_____

_____

_____

_____

_____

_____

_____

_____

_____

_____

_____

_____

_____

_____

_____

_____

_____

_____

_____

_____

Personal Reflections

Note: Write At Least One Positive Affirmation or Scriptural Reference of Gratitude/Abundance. Use Daily Prompts/Resources Provided.

Date: ____/____/____

Personal Reflections

Note: Write At Least One Positive Affirmation or Scriptural Reference of Gratitude/Abundance. Use Daily Prompts/Resources Provided.

Date: ____ / ____ / ____

Personal Reflections

Note: Write At Least One Positive Affirmation or Scriptural Reference of Gratitude/Abundance. Use Daily Prompts/Resources Provided.

Date: ____/____/____

_____

_____

_____

_____

_____

_____

_____

_____

_____

_____

_____

_____

_____

_____

_____

_____

_____

_____

_____

_____

_____

Personal Reflections

Note: Write At Least One Positive Affirmation or Scriptural Reference of Gratitude/Abundance. Use Daily Prompts/Resources Provided.

Date: ____ / ____ / ____

Personal Reflections

Note: Write At Least One Positive Affirmation or Scriptural Reference of Gratitude/Abundance. Use Daily Prompts/Resources Provided.

Date: ____/____/____

Personal Reflections

Note: Write At Least One Positive Affirmation or Scriptural Reference of Gratitude/Abundance. Use Daily Prompts/Resources Provided.

Date: ____/____/____

_____

_____

_____

_____

_____

_____

_____

_____

_____

_____

_____

_____

_____

_____

_____

_____

_____

_____

_____

Personal Reflections

Note: Write At Least One Positive Affirmation or Scriptural Reference of Gratitude/Abundance. Use Daily Prompts/Resources Provided.

Date: ____/____/____

Personal Reflections

Note: Write At Least One Positive Affirmation or Scriptural Reference of Gratitude/Abundance. Use Daily Prompts/Resources Provided.

Date: ____/____/____

_____

_____

_____

_____

_____

_____

_____

_____

_____

_____

_____

_____

_____

_____

_____

_____

_____

_____

_____

_____

Personal Reflections

Note: Write At Least One Positive Affirmation or Scriptural Reference of Gratitude/Abundance. Use Daily Prompts/Resources Provided.

Date: ____/____/____

_____

_____

_____

_____

_____

_____

_____

_____

_____

_____

_____

_____

_____

_____

_____

_____

_____

_____

_____

Personal Reflections

Note: Write At Least One Positive Affirmation or Scriptural Reference of Gratitude/Abundance. Use Daily Prompts/Resources Provided.

Date: _____ / _____ / _____

_____

_____

_____

_____

_____

_____

_____

_____

_____

_____

_____

_____

_____

_____

_____

_____

_____

_____

_____

_____

_____

Personal Reflections

Note: Write At Least One Positive Affirmation or Scriptural Reference of Gratitude/Abundance. Use Daily Prompts/Resources Provided.

Date: ____/____/____

Personal Reflections

Note: Write At Least One Positive Affirmation or Scriptural Reference of Gratitude/Abundance. Use Daily Prompts/Resources Provided.

Date: ____/____/____

_____

_____

_____

_____

_____

_____

_____

_____

_____

_____

_____

_____

_____

_____

_____

_____

_____

_____

_____

_____

Personal Reflections

Note: Write At Least One Positive Affirmation or Scriptural Reference of Gratitude/Abundance. Use Daily Prompts/Resources Provided.

Date: ____/____/____

_____

_____

_____

_____

_____

_____

_____

_____

_____

_____

_____

_____

_____

_____

_____

_____

_____

_____

_____

Personal Reflections

Note: Write At Least One Positive Affirmation or Scriptural Reference of Gratitude/Abundance. Use Daily Prompts/Resources Provided.

Date: ____/____/____

_____

_____

_____

_____

_____

_____

_____

_____

_____

_____

_____

_____

_____

_____

_____

_____

_____

_____

_____

Personal Reflections

Note: Write At Least One Positive Affirmation or Scriptural Reference of Gratitude/Abundance. Use Daily Prompts/Resources Provided.

Date: ____/____/____

_____

_____

_____

_____

_____

_____

_____

_____

_____

_____

_____

_____

_____

_____

_____

_____

_____

_____

_____

_____

Personal Reflections

Note: Write At Least One Positive Affirmation or Scriptural Reference of Gratitude/Abundance. Use Daily Prompts/Resources Provided.

Date: ____/____/____

_____

_____

_____

_____

_____

_____

_____

_____

_____

_____

_____

_____

_____

_____

_____

_____

_____

_____

_____

Personal Reflections

Note: Write At Least One Positive Affirmation or Scriptural Reference of Gratitude/Abundance. Use Daily Prompts/Resources Provided.

Date: ____/____/____

_____

_____

_____

_____

_____

_____

_____

_____

_____

_____

_____

_____

_____

_____

_____

_____

_____

_____

_____

_____

Personal Reflections

Note: Write At Least One Positive Affirmation or Scriptural Reference of Gratitude/Abundance. Use Daily Prompts/Resources Provided.

Date: ____/____/____

Note: Write At Least One Positive Affirmation or Scriptural Reference of Gratitude/Abundance. Use Daily Prompts/Resources Provided.

Date: ____/____/____

_____

_____

_____

_____

_____

_____

_____

_____

_____

_____

_____

_____

_____

_____

_____

_____

_____

_____

_____

_____

Personal Reflections

Note: Write At Least One Positive Affirmation or Scriptural Reference of Gratitude/Abundance. Use Daily Prompts/Resources Provided.

Date: ____/____/____

_____

_____

_____

_____

_____

_____

_____

_____

_____

_____

_____

_____

_____

_____

_____

_____

_____

_____

_____

_____

Personal Reflections

Note: Write At Least One Positive Affirmation or Scriptural Reference of Gratitude/Abundance. Use Daily Prompts/Resources Provided.

Date: ____/____/____

_____

_____

_____

_____

_____

_____

_____

_____

_____

_____

_____

_____

_____

_____

_____

_____

_____

_____

_____

_____

_____

Personal Reflections

Note: Write At Least One Positive Affirmation or Scriptural Reference of Gratitude/Abundance. Use Daily Prompts/Resources Provided.

Date: ____ / ____ / ____

_____

_____

_____

_____

_____

_____

_____

_____

_____

_____

_____

_____

_____

_____

_____

_____

_____

_____

_____

Personal Reflections

Note: Write At Least One Positive Affirmation or Scriptural Reference of Gratitude/Abundance. Use Daily Prompts/Resources Provided.

Date: ____/____/____

_____

_____

_____

_____

_____

_____

_____

_____

_____

_____

_____

_____

_____

_____

_____

_____

_____

_____

_____

_____

_____

Personal Reflections

Note: Write At Least One Positive Affirmation or Scriptural Reference of Gratitude/Abundance. Use Daily Prompts/Resources Provided.

Date: ____/____/____

_____

_____

_____

_____

_____

_____

_____

_____

_____

_____

_____

_____

_____

_____

_____

_____

_____

_____

Note: Write At Least One Positive Affirmation or Scriptural Reference of Gratitude/Abundance. Use Daily Prompts/Resources Provided.

Date: ____/____/____

_____

_____

_____

_____

_____

_____

_____

_____

_____

_____

_____

_____

_____

_____

_____

_____

_____

_____

_____

_____

_____

_____

Personal Reflections

Note: Write At Least One Positive Affirmation or Scriptural Reference of Gratitude/Abundance. Use Daily Prompts/Resources Provided.

Date: ____ / ____ / ____

_____

_____

_____

_____

_____

_____

_____

_____

_____

_____

_____

_____

_____

_____

_____

_____

_____

_____

_____

_____

_____

Personal Reflections

Note: Write At Least One Positive Affirmation or Scriptural Reference of Gratitude/Abundance. Use Daily Prompts/Resources Provided.

Date: ____ / ____ / ____

_____

_____

_____

_____

_____

_____

_____

_____

_____

_____

_____

_____

_____

_____

_____

_____

_____

_____

_____

_____

_____

_____

_____

Daily Prompts

Morning Prompts:

- What/Who Am I Grateful For and Why?
- How Can I Serve/Pour Into Others?
- What Is At Least One Thing I Can Do To Walk In Purpose Today?
- Write One Scripture to Meditate On.
- Write One Positive Affirmation, Repeat It Aloud.

Evening Prompts:

- What/Who Am I Grateful For and Why?
- What/Who Motivated Me On Today? How?
- What/Who Inspired Me On Today? How?
- Who Did I Serve? What Impact did this have on me?
- Who Did I Pour Into Mentally, Emotionally, Spiritually? In what ways? How did this impact me?
- Who Poured Into Me Mentally, Emotionally, Spiritually? In what ways? How did this impact me?
- Did I Show Myself Love On Today? If So, In What Ways?
- Did I Work On My Goals Pertaining To My Purpose And/Or Vision? What action steps can I take in the future?
- Reflecting On Today, What Can I Do Differently Tomorrow To Aid In My Growth As An Individual?
- Write One Scripture to Meditate On.
- Write One Positive Affirmation, Repeat It Aloud.

Daily Positive Affirmations

1. I am whole.
2. I am gifted.
3. I am healed.
4. I am courageous.
5. I am wealthy.
6. I walk in wisdom and knowledge.
7. I am well mind, body, spirit.
8. I am optimistic, releasing all fear.
9. The relationships in my life add to my growth as an individual.
10. I live a rich and fulfilled life in all the areas of my life.
11. I am beautiful.
12. I live in abundance, and because of my abundance I can freely give to others.
13. I am loved, I give love, love surrounds me.
14. I flow in positive energy, and only positive energy surrounds me.
15. I walk in power.
16. I am grateful.
17. I release all that is keeping me from walking in my full potential and purpose.
18. I let go of all toxic relationships in my life.
19. I live guilt-free.
20. I am in control of my happiness, and I choose to live in joy and peace.
21. I am forgiven.
22. I forgive those who have hurt me, and I am walking in love and peace.
23. I am worthy.
24. I believe in myself and can accomplish what I set my mind to.
25. I am unique, and I celebrate my individuality.
26. I am prepared to succeed and to walk in purpose.
27. I forgive myself for past mistakes.
28. I release bitterness and anger.
29. I know that life is a journey, and I choose to learn from my experiences along the way.
30. My life is a gift, and I am thankful.

Scriptural References of Gratitude and Abundance

1. Rejoice always, pray continually, give thanks in all circumstances; for this is God's will for you in Christ - 1 Thessalonians 5:16-18

2. Do not be anxious about anything, but in every situation, by prayer and petition, with thanksgiving, present your requests to God. And the peace of God, which transcends all understanding, will guard your hearts and your minds in Christ Jesus. -Philippians 4:6-7

3. Devote yourselves to prayer, being watchful and thankful. ~ Col. 4:2

4. But thanks be to God! He gives us the victory through our Lord Jesus Christ. - 1 Corinthians 15:57

5. We ought always to thank God for you, brothers and sisters, and rightly so, because your faith is growing more and more, and the love all of you have for one another is increasing. ~ 2 Thessalonians 1:3

6. Let the peace of Christ rule in your hearts, since as members of one body you were called to peace. And be thankful. – Col. 3:15

7. Give thanks to the Lord, for he is good; his love endures forever. - 1 Chronicles 16:34

8. For from him and through him and for him are all things. To him be the glory forever! Amen.- Romans 11:36

9. Then I heard every creature in heaven and on earth and under the earth and on the sea, and all that is in them, saying: "To him who sits on the throne and to the Lamb be praise and honor and glory and power, forever and ever!" - Revelation 5:13

10. I will give thanks to you, Lord, with all my heart; I will tell of all your wonderful deeds. – Ps. 9:1

11. Let the message of Christ dwell among you richly as you teach and admonish one another with all wisdom through psalms, hymns, and songs from the Spirit, singing to God with gratitude in your hearts.- Col. 3:16

12. You will be enriched in every way so that you can be generous on every occasion, and through us your generosity will result in thanksgiving to God.- 2 Cor. 9:11

13. And whatever you do, whether in word or deed, do it all in the name of the Lord Jesus, giving thanks to God the Father through him. – Col. 3:17

14. But I, with shouts of grateful praise, will sacrifice to you. What I have vowed I will make good. I will say, 'Salvation comes from the Lord. - Jonah 2:9

15. O Come, let us sing for joy to the Lord; Let us shout joyfully to the rock of our salvation. Let us come into his presence with thanksgiving; let us make a joyful noise to him with songs of

praise! For the Lord is a great God, and a great King above all gods. ~ Ps. 95:1~3

16. Enter his gates with thanksgiving, and his courts with praise! Give thanks to him; bless his name! For the Lord is good; his steadfast love endures forever, and his faithfulness to all generations. ~ Ps. 100:4~5

17. Give thanks to the Lord for he is good, his love endures forever. ~ Ps. 118:29

18. I will give thanks to you, LORD, with all my heart; I will tell of all your wonderful deeds.~ Ps. 9:1

19. I will give to the Lord the thanks due to his righteousness, and I will sing praise to the name of the Lord, the Most High. ~ Ps. 7:17

20. Let your roots grow down into him, and let your lives be built on him. Then your faith will grow strong in the truth you were taught, and you will overflow with thankfulness. ~ Col. 2:7

21. And let the peace of Christ rule in your hearts, to which indeed you were called in one body; and be thankful. ~ Col. 3:15

22. Devote yourselves to prayer, being watchful and thankful. ~ Col. 4:2

23. I will praise the name of God with song, and shall magnify him with Thanksgiving ~ Ps. 69:30

24. Bless the Lord, O my soul, and all that is within me, bless his holy name! Bless the Lord, O my soul, and forget not all his benefits, who forgives all your iniquity, who heals all your diseases, who redeems your life from the pit, who crowns you with steadfast love and mercy, who satisfies you with good so that your youth is renewed like the eagle's. ~ Ps. 103:1~5

25. Give thanks in all circumstances; for this is the will of God in Christ Jesus for you.~ 1 Thess. 5:18

26. Oh give thanks to the Lord, for he is good, for his steadfast love endures forever! ~ Ps. 107:1

27. Giving thanks always and for everything to God the Father in the name of our Lord Jesus Christ ~ Eph. 5:20

28. The Lord is my strength and my shield; My heart trusts in Him, and I am helped; Therefore my heart exults, And with my song I shall thank Him. ~ Ps. 28:7

29. Thanks be to God for his inexpressible gift! – 2 Cor. 9:15

30. Give thanks to the Lord, for he is good, for his steadfast love endures forever. Give thanks to the God of gods, for his steadfast love endures forever. Give thanks to the Lord of lords, for his steadfast love endures forever; to him who alone does great wonders, for his steadfast love endures forever; to him who by understanding made the heavens, for his steadfast love endures forever ~ Ps. 136:1~5

Memories: Photos/Drawings Here

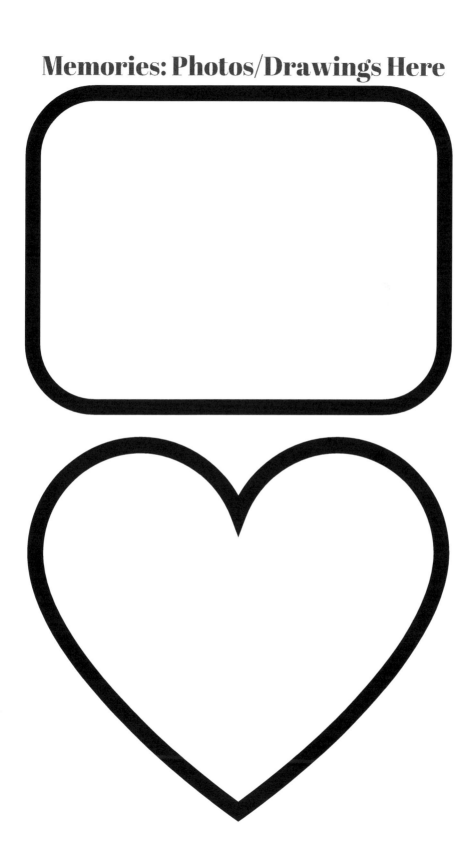

Memories: Photos/Drawings Here

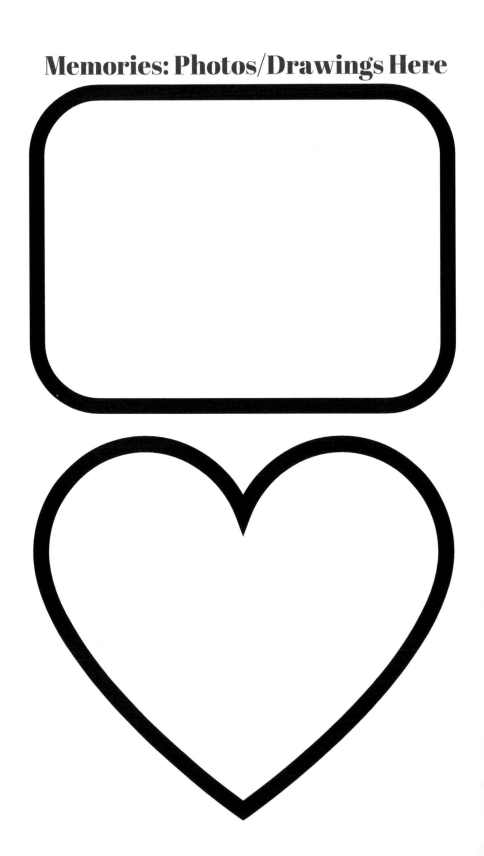

Memories: Photos/Drawings Here

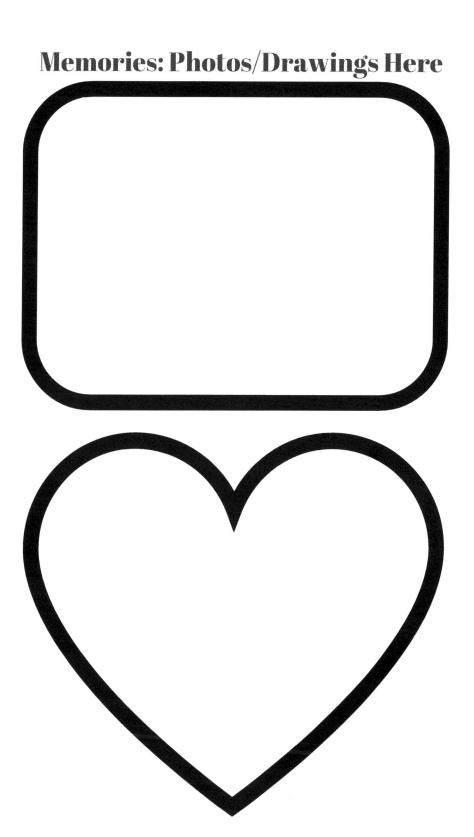

Memories: Photos/Drawings Here

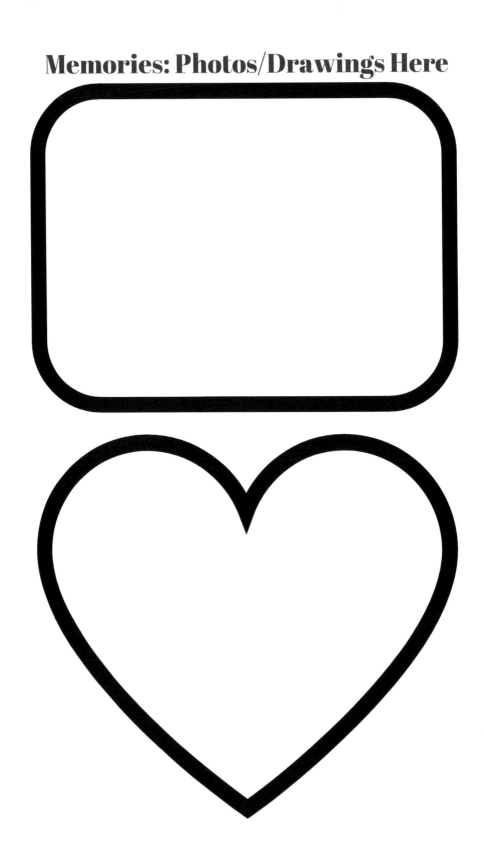

Memories: Photos/Drawings Here

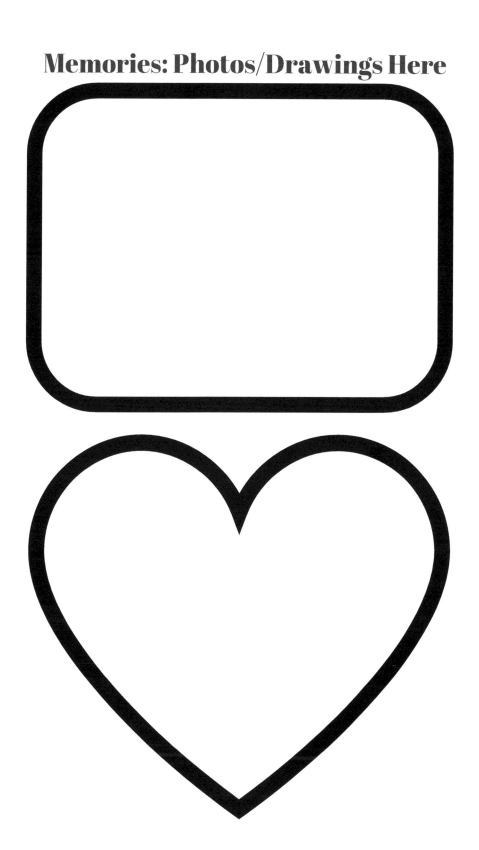

Memories: Photos/Drawings Here

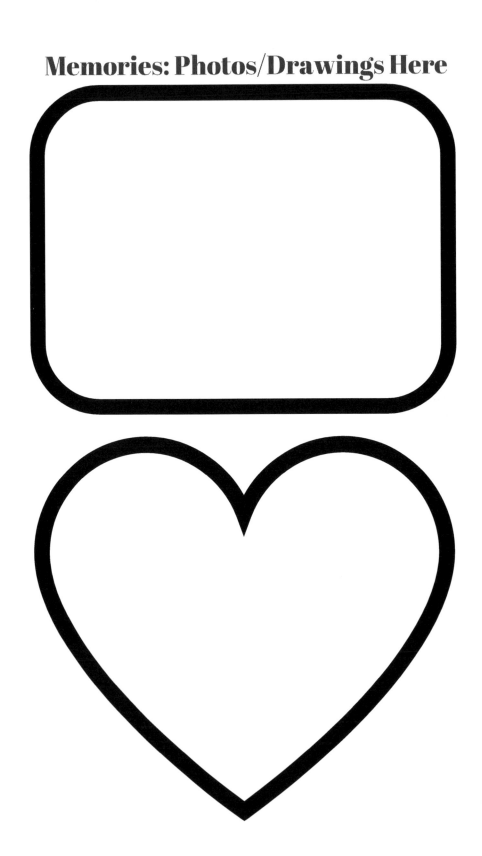

Memories: Photos/Drawings Here

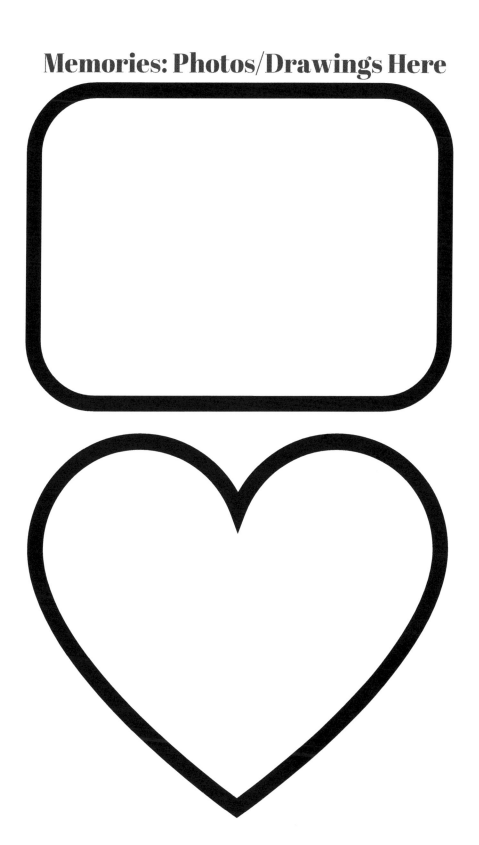

Memories: Photos/Drawings Here

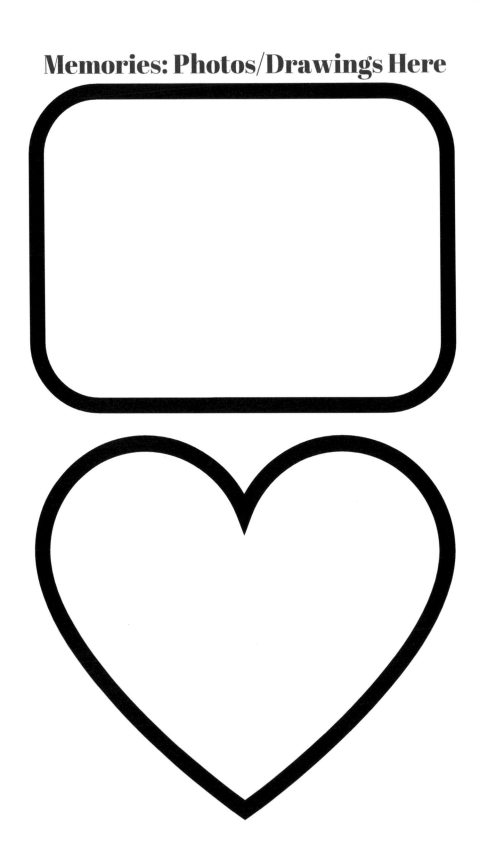

Memories: Photos/Drawings Here

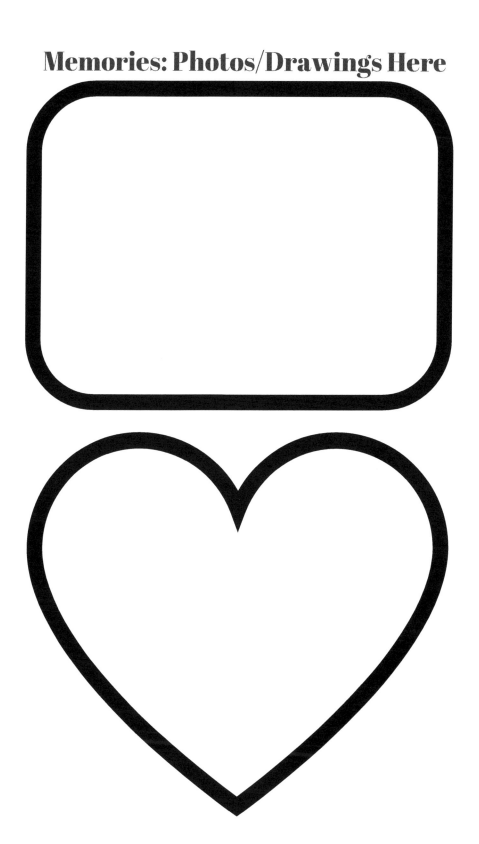

Memories: Photos/Drawings Here

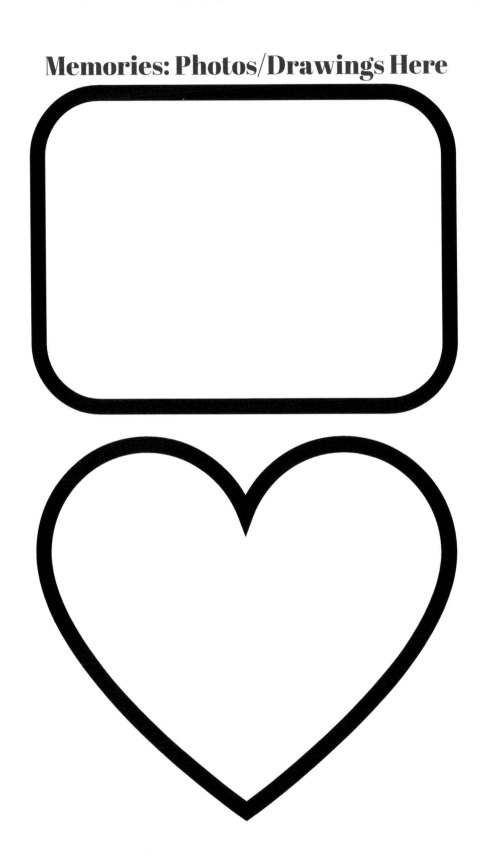

Memories: Photos/Drawings Here

Memories: Photos/Drawings Here

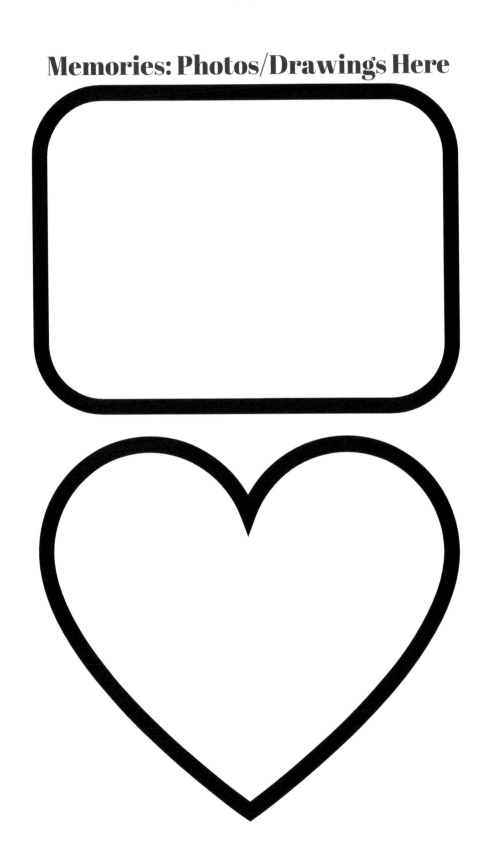

Made in the USA
Columbia, SC
17 April 2019